May Gibbs
Gumnut Babies™
TREASURY

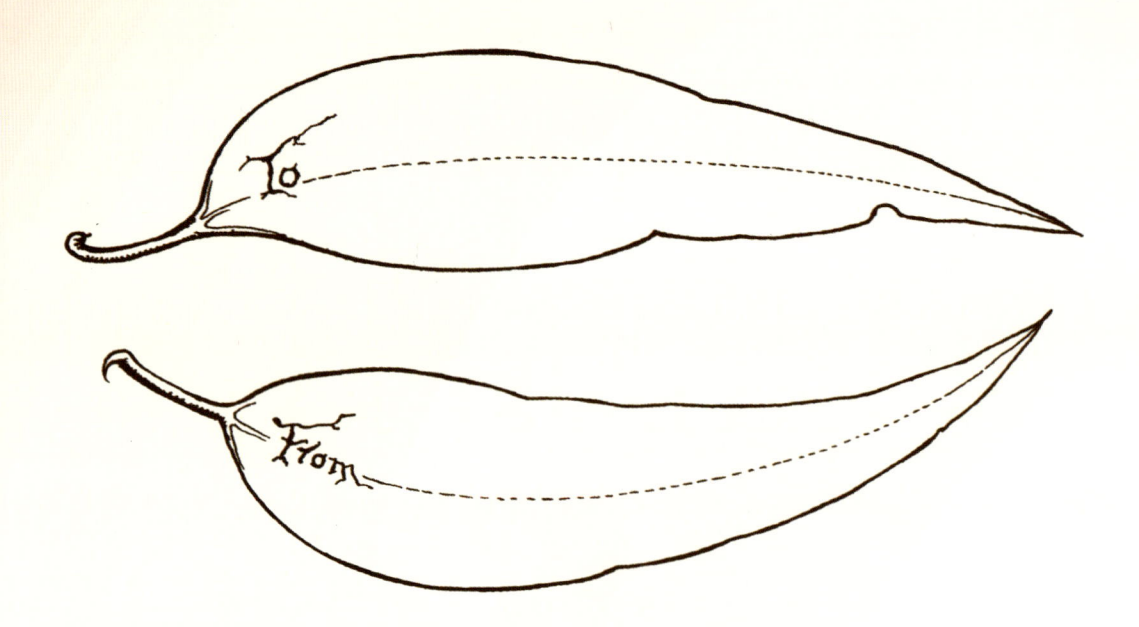

Scholastic Australia Pty Limited
PO Box 579 Gosford NSW 2250
ABN 11 000 614 577
www.scholastic.com.au

Part of the Scholastic Group
Sydney • Auckland • New York • Toronto • London • Mexico City
New Delhi • Hong Kong • Buenos Aires • Puerto Rico

Gumnut Babies first published in Australia in 1916.
Gum-Blossom Babies first published in Australia in 1916.
Flannel Flowers and Other Bush Babies first published in Australia in 1917.
Boronia Babies first published in Australia in 1917.
Wattle Babies first published in Australia in 1918.

This edition published by Scholastic Australia in 2020.
Page 27 has been updated from the original text as it contained outdated cultural depictions.

This combined edition copyright © The Northcott Society and Cerebral Palsy Alliance 2020.

All rights reserved. No part of this publication may be reproduced or transmitted in any form or by any means, electronic or mechanical, including photocopying, recording, storage in an information retrieval system, or otherwise, without the prior written permission of the publisher, unless specifically permitted under the Australian Copyright Act 1968 as amended.

A catalogue record for this book is available from the National Library of Australia

ISBN 978-1-76097-832-7

Typeset in Cantoria MT.

Printed in China by RR Donnelley.

Scholastic Australia's policy, in association with RR Donnelley, is to use papers that are renewable and made efficiently from wood grown in responsibly managed forests, so as to minimise its environmental footprint.

Part of the proceeds help to assist the work of Cerebral Palsy Alliance of New South Wales,
187 Allambie Road, Allambie Heights, NSW 2100, www.cerebralpalsy.org.au and
The Northcott Society, 1 Fennell Street, North Parramatta, NSW 2151, www.northcott.com.au

For more information on May Gibbs please visit www.maygibbs.org

10 9 8 7 6 5   21 22 23 24 / 2

May Gibbs Gumnut Babies™ TREASURY

A Scholastic Australia Book

CONTENTS

Gumnut Babies 1

Gum-Blossom Babies 25

Flannel Flowers and Other Bush Babies.........................49

Boronia Babies..73

Wattle Babies 97

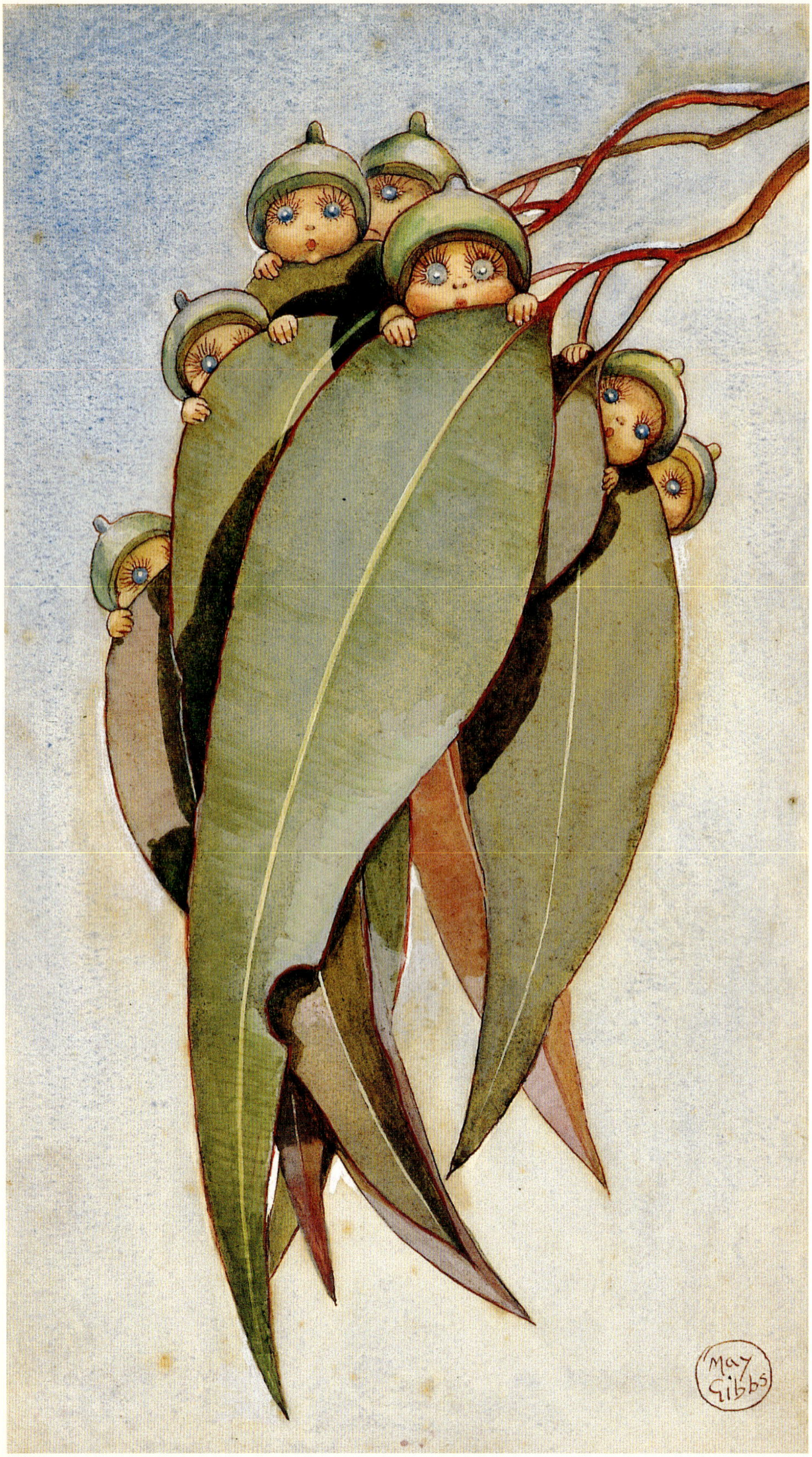
May
Gibbs

Gumnut Babies

Words and Pictures by May Gibbs

May Gibbs

Where They Live

On all the big Gumtrees there are Gumnut Babies. Some people see them and some don't; but they see everybody and everything. Possibly, that's how their eyes have grown so big.

May Gibbs

A Habit of Theirs

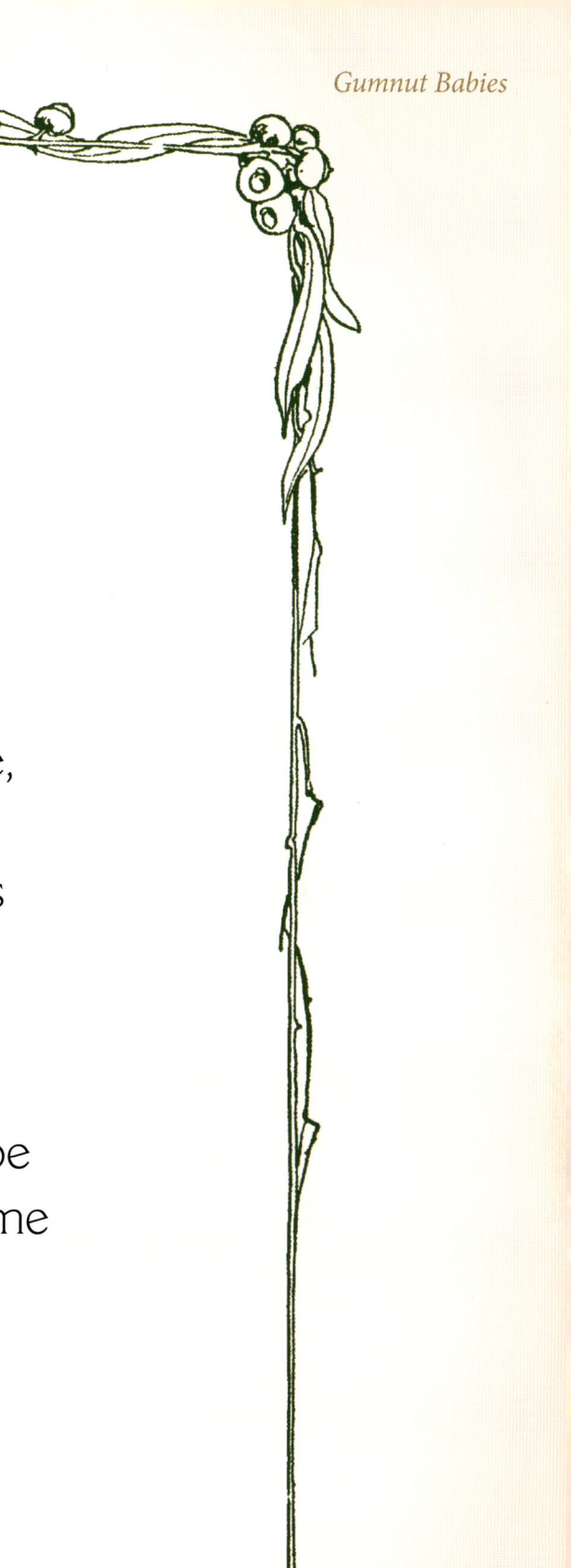

They love to sit in the sunshine, warming various parts of themselves while they think. They think of everything and wonder why; maybe that's how they came to look so solemn.

May Gibbs

Fearless

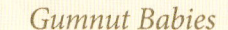

When the wind blows high, they ride the tossing boughs and shout; that is how they learn the art of never falling. Only the grown-up Nuts can take off their caps.

May Gibbs

Like Little Pucks

They are full of mischief and are always teasing the slow-going creatures; but they hurt nothing and are gentle, for they love all the world.

May Gibbs

So Neighbourly

In the Springtime, when birds are busy with their nests, the little Nuts do all they can to help them; they love the baby birds as if they were their own.

May Gibbs

Such Tender Hearts

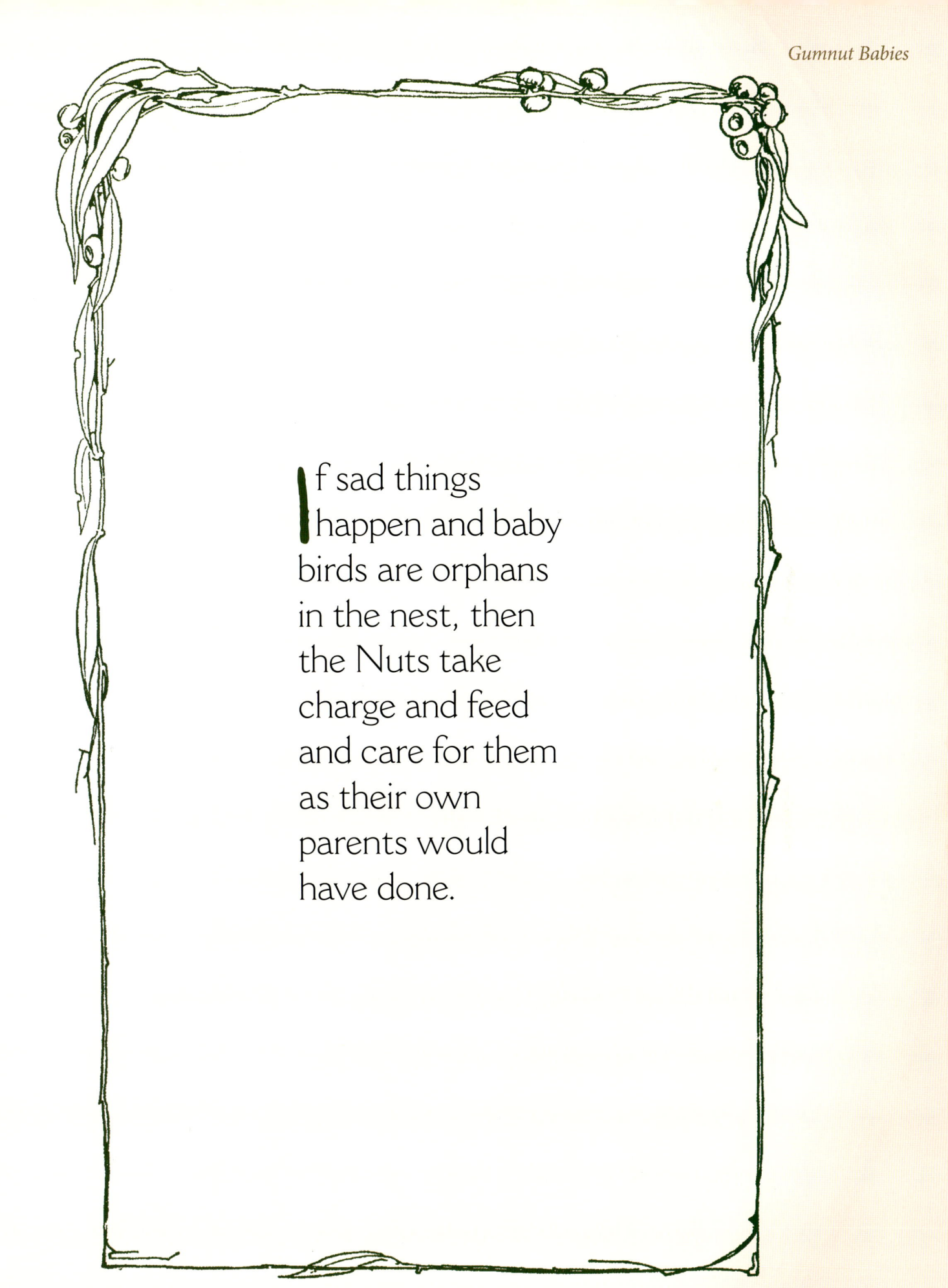

If sad things happen and baby birds are orphans in the nest, then the Nuts take charge and feed and care for them as their own parents would have done.

May Gibbs

Full of Sympathy

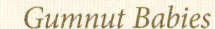

Once, when poor Mrs Possum lost her only child, one of the little Nuts climbed into her pouch and pretended to be her baby. Mrs Possum was so much comforted.

May Gibbs

They Try So Hard

16

It vexes the little Nuts that they cannot hang by their tails like baby possums do; it would be so very convenient.

May Gibbs

Great Friends

Perhaps, of all the folk in the Bush, Mrs Kookaburra is most fond of the Nuts. They amuse her, they make her laugh. Mrs Kookaburra's laugh is a little cynical; but then, she eats so many snakes.

Sometimes Afraid

Though the Nuts are friends with all the Bush Folk and love all the world, they are just a little afraid of lizards and snakes; but even the wickedest snake wouldn't hurt a Nut.

When They Sleep

At noonday, when the sun is warm, and at night, when the frogs are singing, they hang their heavy heads over their swaying leaves and sleep.

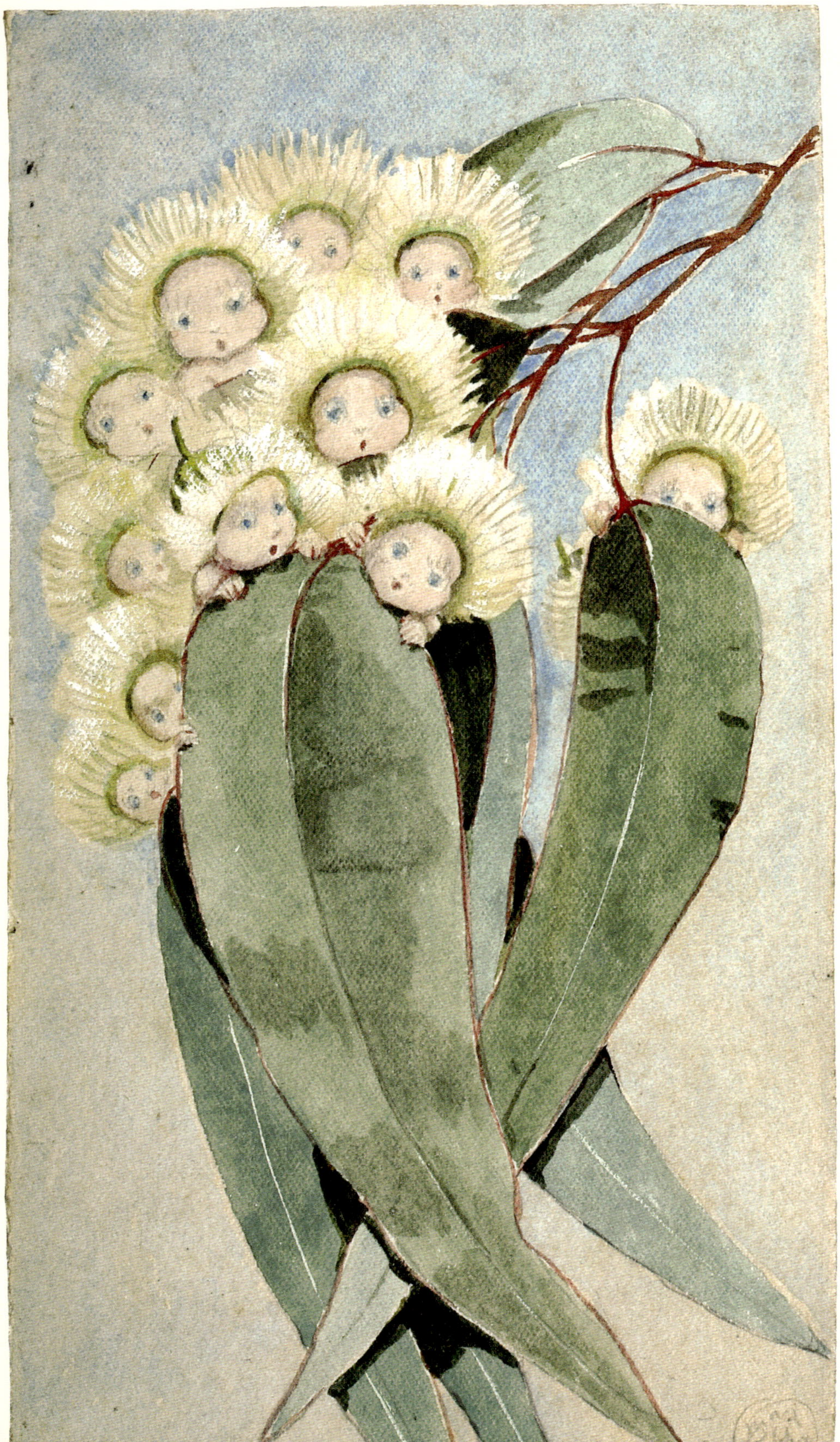

Words and Pictures

Gum Blossom Babies

by May Gibbs

May Gibbs

In Their Homes

Gum-Blossom Babies are much harder to find than Gumnut Babies. They are more timid and are generally clustered together in their homes on the tops of the trees.

May Gibbs

New Frocks Every Spring

So sweet is the scent of their frocks, and so like real blossoms do they look, that Mr Bee often makes a blunder and settles upon the hat of a startled little person.

May Gibbs

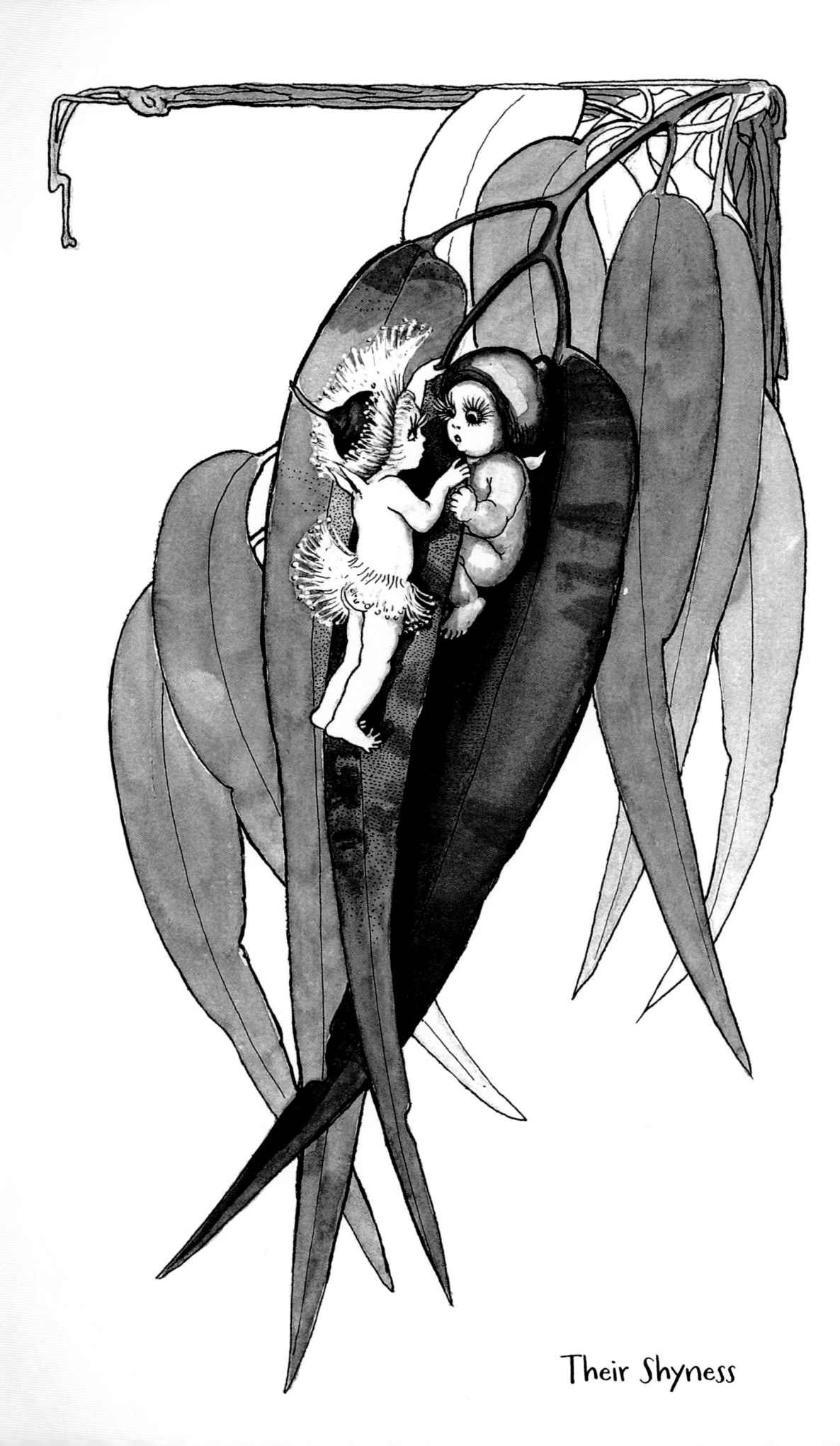

Their Shyness

It mostly happens that Nuts and Blossoms see very little of one another; so when they meet they are rather shy, but very interested.

May Gibbs

Lovers of Music

Gum-Blossom Babies

When Signor Cicada gives a recital all the Blossom Babies crowd in, but scarcely a Nut will appear.

May Gibbs

Tender Hearts

Blossom Babies, like the Nuts, love all the Bush Folk, and are even more tender-hearted. It distresses them that spiders will eat flies, so they rescue them when they can. Maybe that's why there are so many flies.

May Gibbs

Like Big Humans

They take much interest in their neighbours' affairs and love to talk—how many snakes Mrs Kookaburra had for breakfast—how Mr Possum was stuck up the wrong tree all night by a dog—how Mrs Wagtail's nest was robbed—and such gossip.

Their Little Babies

In the Buds—that's where the Babies are found—the lids lift up, the petals quickly unfold, and the Baby is tossed out into the arms of the expectant little Mother. She has waited and watched, for she knows which bud holds a Baby.

May Gibbs

In the Nursery

Very little Babies are fed with honey and dew, and are carefully nursed till their caps grow big.

May Gibbs

Those Important Caps

When the Babies' caps grow big, then they can climb alone. If they fall, their heads being large and heavy, they go head first, and their thick, soft caps protect them.

May Gibbs

Great Adventures

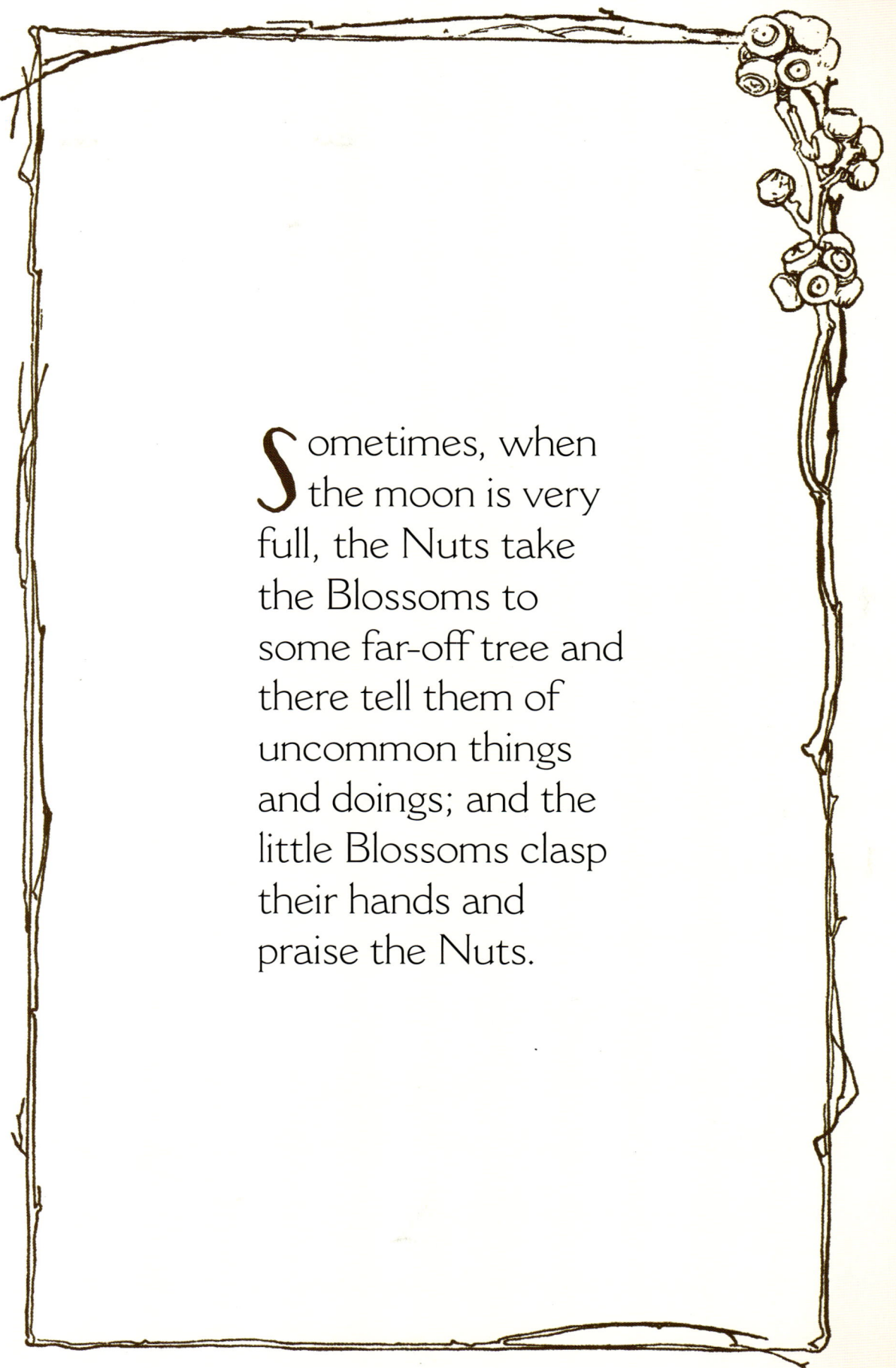

Sometimes, when the moon is very full, the Nuts take the Blossoms to some far-off tree and there tell them of uncommon things and doings; and the little Blossoms clasp their hands and praise the Nuts.

May Gibbs

Sleeping Time

When twilight deepens into dark, and the last tint of sun has stolen from the distant hill, the little Blossoms fold their petals about them and close their eyes in sleep.

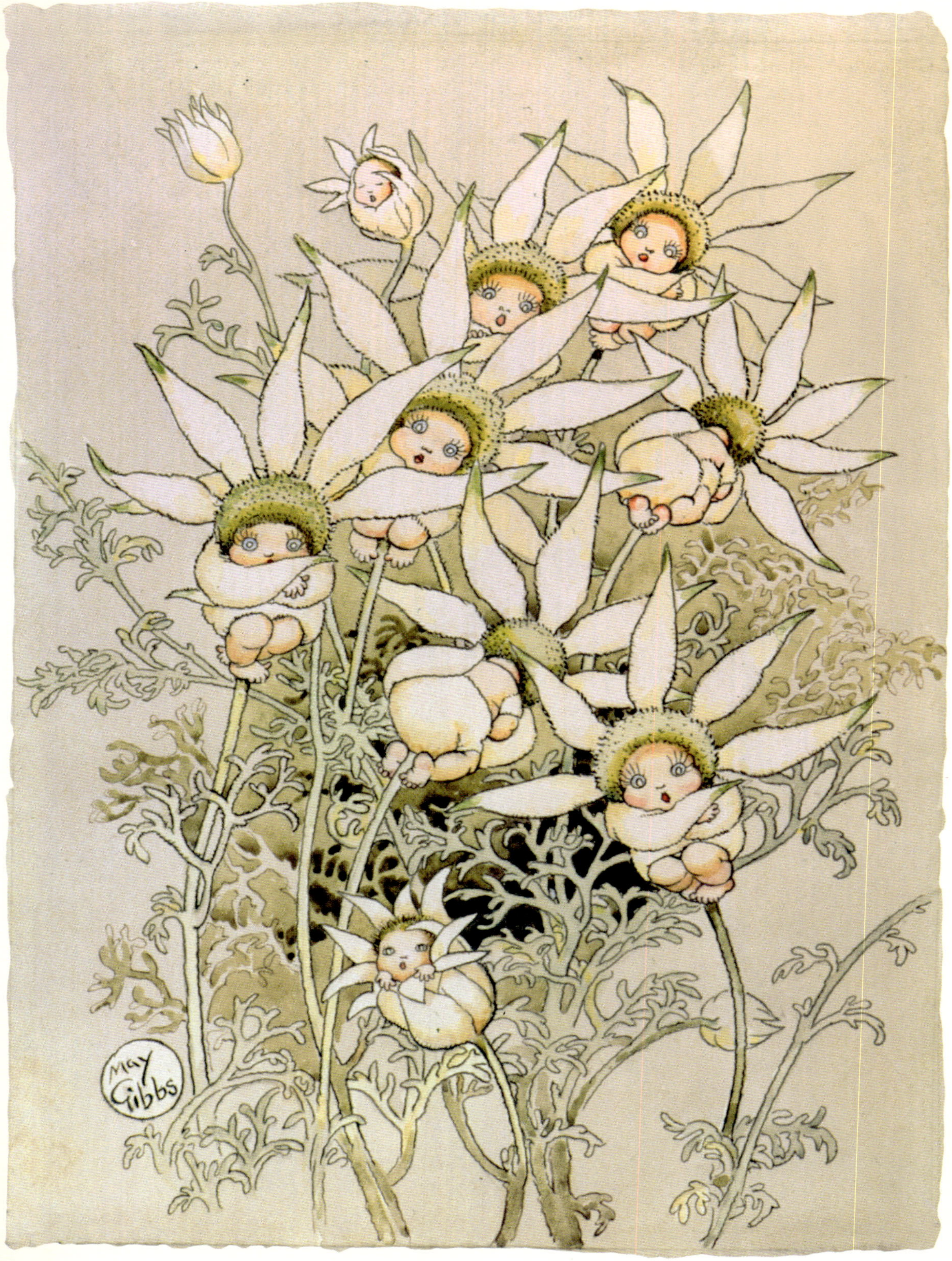
May Gibbs

Flannel Flowers and Other Bush Babies

May Gibbs

May Gibbs

Young Flannel Babies

Flannel Flowers and Other Bush Babies

As Summer days grow warmer, countless little soft Flannel Babies come out of their buds and sit swaying about on their long green stems. Perhaps you've seen them?

May Gibbs

Quite Grown Up

Flannel Flowers and Other Bush Babies

These older ones are feeding a sad little Baby Bird. He is lost and hungry—but it's a pity about the poor worm, isn't it?

When the Moon is Round

Flannel Flowers and Other Bush Babies

Almost any evening, when the Moon is round and the night is still, these little figures may be seen whirling over the glossy surface of a big Gum leaf.

May Gibbs

Christmas Bell Babies

Flannel Flowers and Other Bush Babies

Christmas Bell Babies are frisky, jolly little chaps. They love, above all things, to play leapfrog with their friends from the creek.

May Gibbs

Dragon-flying

Flannel Flowers and Other Bush Babies

Only the very daring ones go Dragon-flying. The more timid only cheer them and admire them greatly.

May Gibbs

Bracken Fern Babies

Flannel Flowers and Other Bush Babies

Have you ever noticed the Bracken Babies? They know all about Mrs Snake and can tell the strangest stories of her sly doings.

May Gibbs

Yellow Pea-flower Babies

Then there are the Pea-flower Babies. In the early Spring they are everywhere, making the Bush happy with their gay yellow hats.

May Gibbs

Mushroom Babies

Flannel Flowers and Other Bush Babies

When you are walking in the fields be very careful not to step on these funny little fellows. Whatever you do, don't mistake them for Mushrooms and have them cooked for breakfast.

May Gibbs

Native Fuchsia Babies

Flannel Flowers and Other Bush Babies

Very quaint and shy are the Native Fuchsia Babies—they run about together, holding hands and balancing carefully because of their long red and white caps.

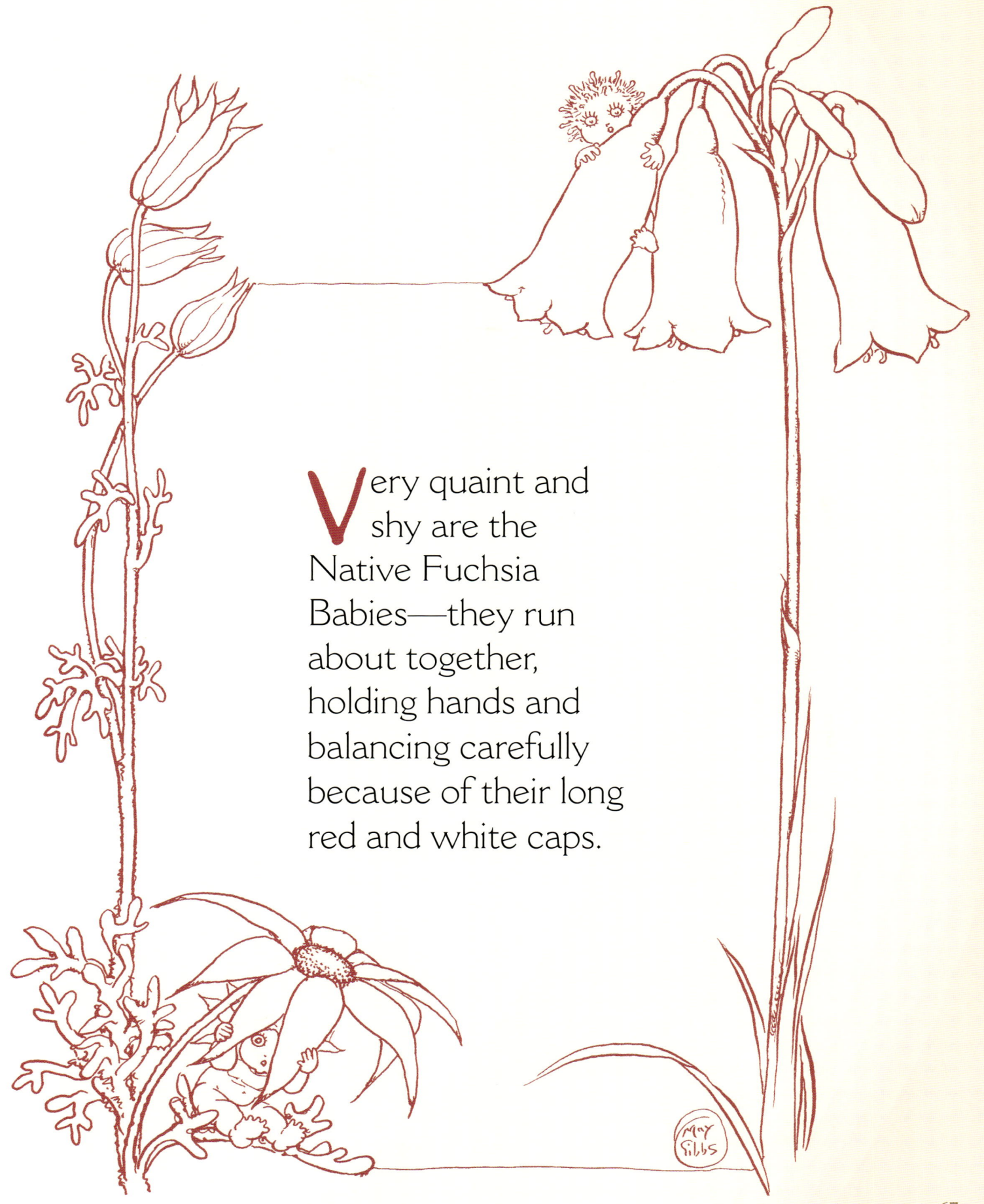

May Gibbs

The Ti-tree Babies

Flannel Flowers and Other Bush Babies

Nothing is prettier than a row of pink and white Ti-tree Babies, swinging on a grey stem with their dainty hats spread like wings in the sunshine.

Asleep

Flannel Flowers and Other Bush Babies

When the Sun has gone and the big Stars come out one by one, all the Bush Babies fall asleep and stir not till the morning chatter of the Early Birds wakes them to another day.

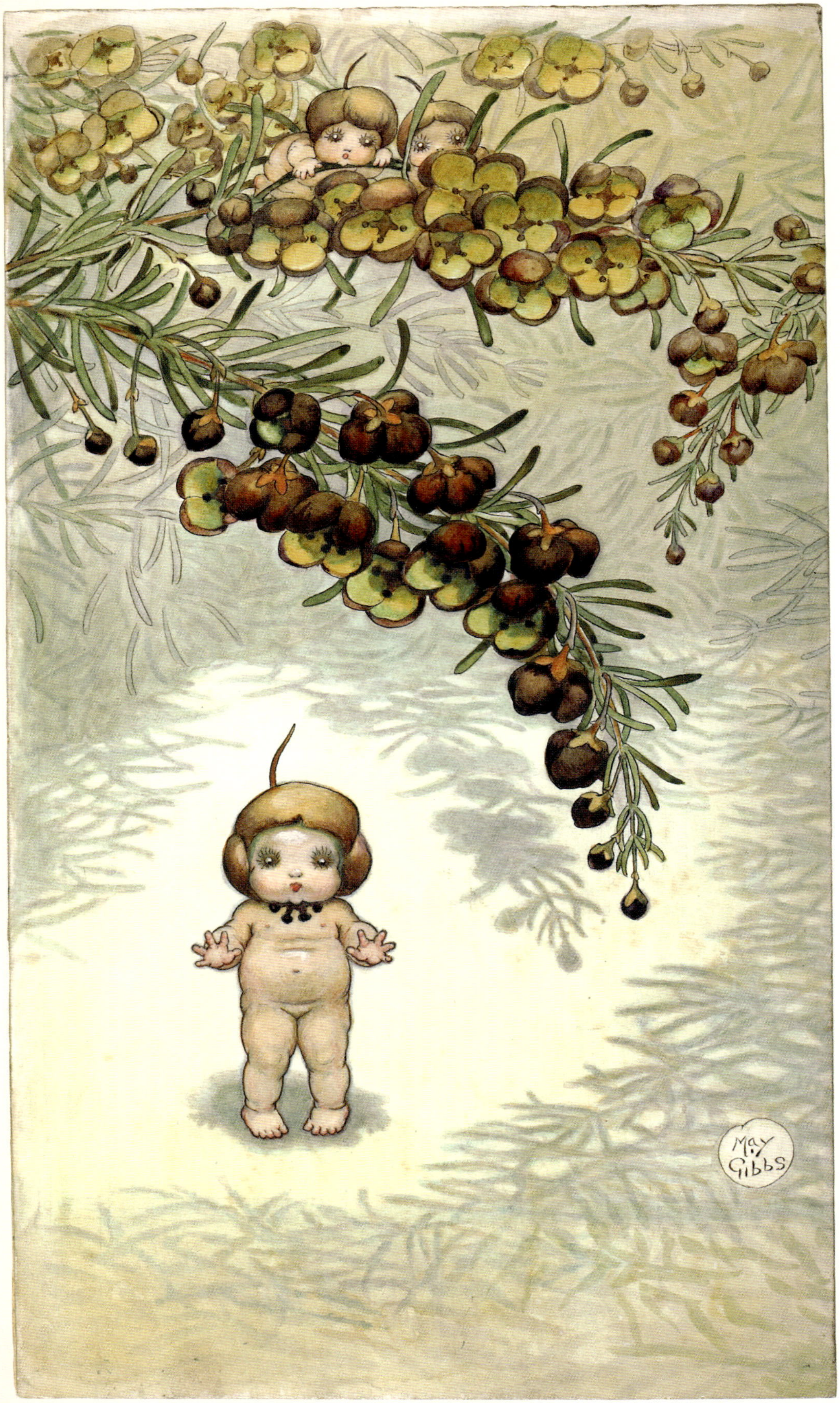
May Gibbs

Boronia Babies

May Gibbs

May Gibbs

TRESPASSERS will be eaten

May Gibbs

A Scent Factory

Boronia Babies

Little Brown Boronias are very dear to all the Bush people because not only are they gentle and sweet, but they wear a most delicious scent. Here they are making some; it is their secret, and while they work big Mr Spider keeps watch against intruders.

Finding Babies

Boronia Babies

These are Native Rose Babies. They are second cousins to the Pale Pink Boronias, and are considered rather eccentric by their friends. See the little mothers hurrying to get their babies; if they are not quick the Buds will open right out and the babies will fall down and die.

May Gibbs

The Acrobat

The Brown Boronia Babies are wonderful Acrobats. Here is one keeping his audience spellbound with his antics. The careful Spiders have a web spread below to catch him if he falls.

Joy-riding

In return for a little drop of scent, Butterflies will carry the Boronias about for hours. The Babies are very fond of flying, and are especially proud of the gaudy colours of their 'buses'.

May Gibbs

Flying

Boronia Babies

Pink Boronia Babies go sailing in the sunshine with pink parachutes. This is a game they love beyond all others. Sometimes Ants and Beetles try to fly too, and go tumbling to the ground, which greatly amuses the little Bush people.

May Gibbs

See-saw

84

Boronia Babies

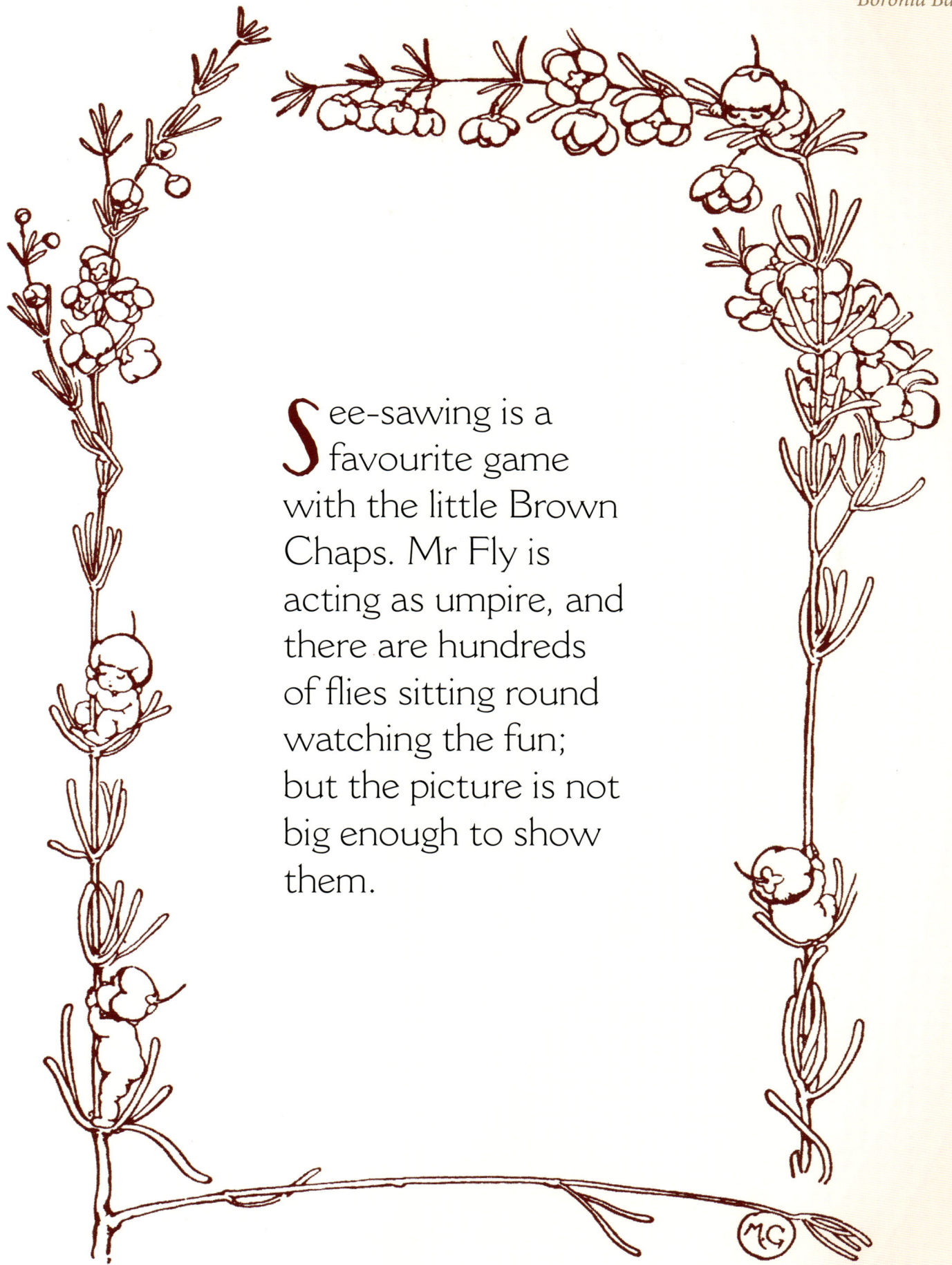

See-sawing is a favourite game with the little Brown Chaps. Mr Fly is acting as umpire, and there are hundreds of flies sitting round watching the fun; but the picture is not big enough to show them.

May Gibbs

Going on a Journey

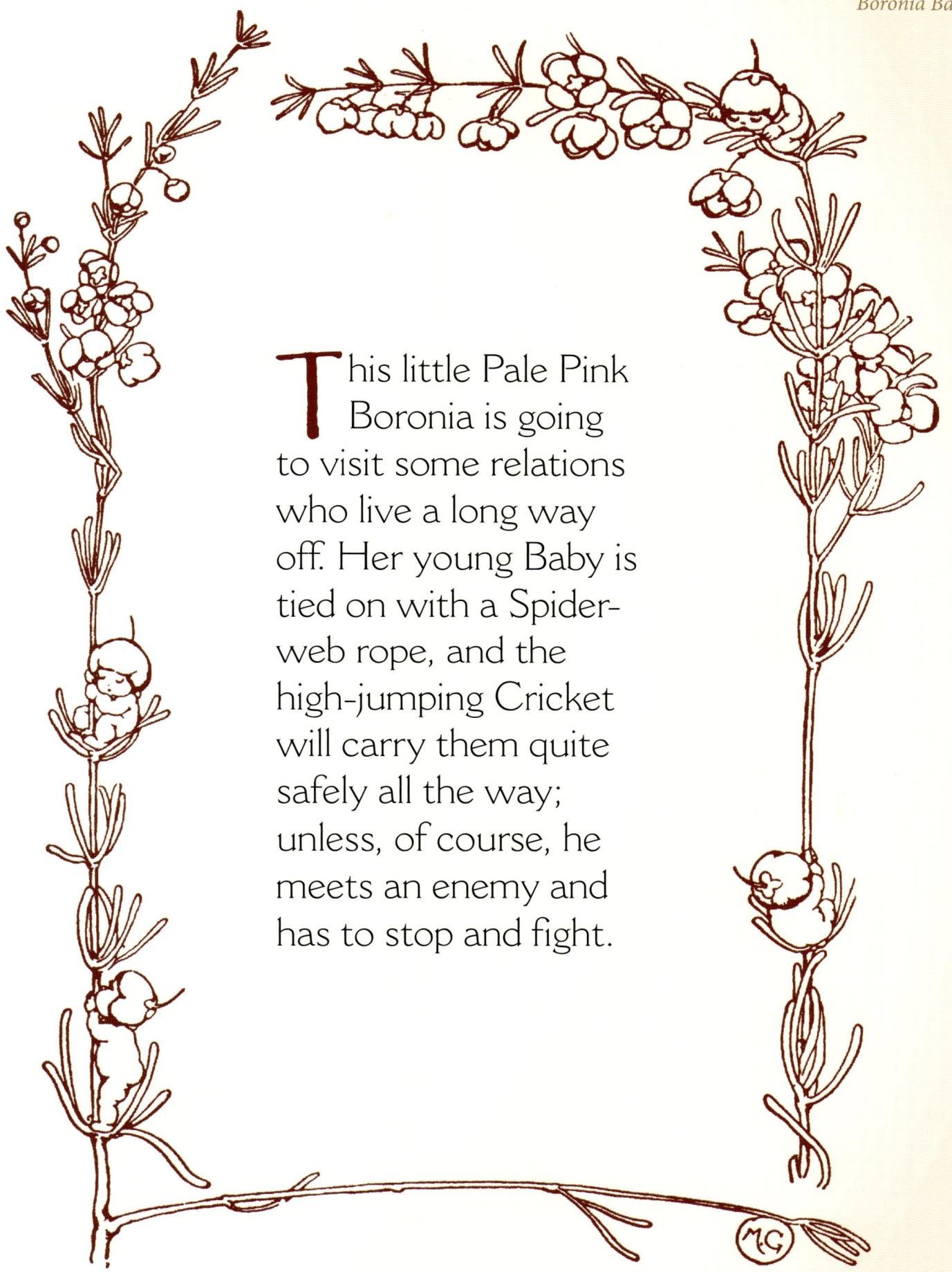

This little Pale Pink Boronia is going to visit some relations who live a long way off. Her young Baby is tied on with a Spider-web rope, and the high-jumping Cricket will carry them quite safely all the way; unless, of course, he meets an enemy and has to stop and fight.

May Gibbs

Swinging

Boronia Babies

Spiders are great friends with the Boronia Babies. They make fine strong swings for them, and even swing the very little ones, as you see in the picture. Two more are anxiously waiting for their turns.

May Gibbs

The Shivery Dance

Boronia Babies

Here are two small Brown Boronias watching some Grass Babies dancing their Shivery Dance. They quiver and quake and jump and shake till the petals of the Boronia Babies stand right up on end with astonishment.

May Gibbs

Shadows

Boronia Babies

The Bush is always full of shadows, especially on bright moonlight nights. This little Boronia Baby is very brave and comes out all alone, long before the Brown Babies, and Pink Babies, and Native Rose Babies are awake. The shadows look terrible, but they wouldn't really hurt anyone.

May Gibbs

Bedtime

Boronia Babies

At night the Mothers put their little Babies to sleep under Spider nets so that they may rest undisturbed by the busy night-flying creatures who come hunting for scent under cover of darkness.

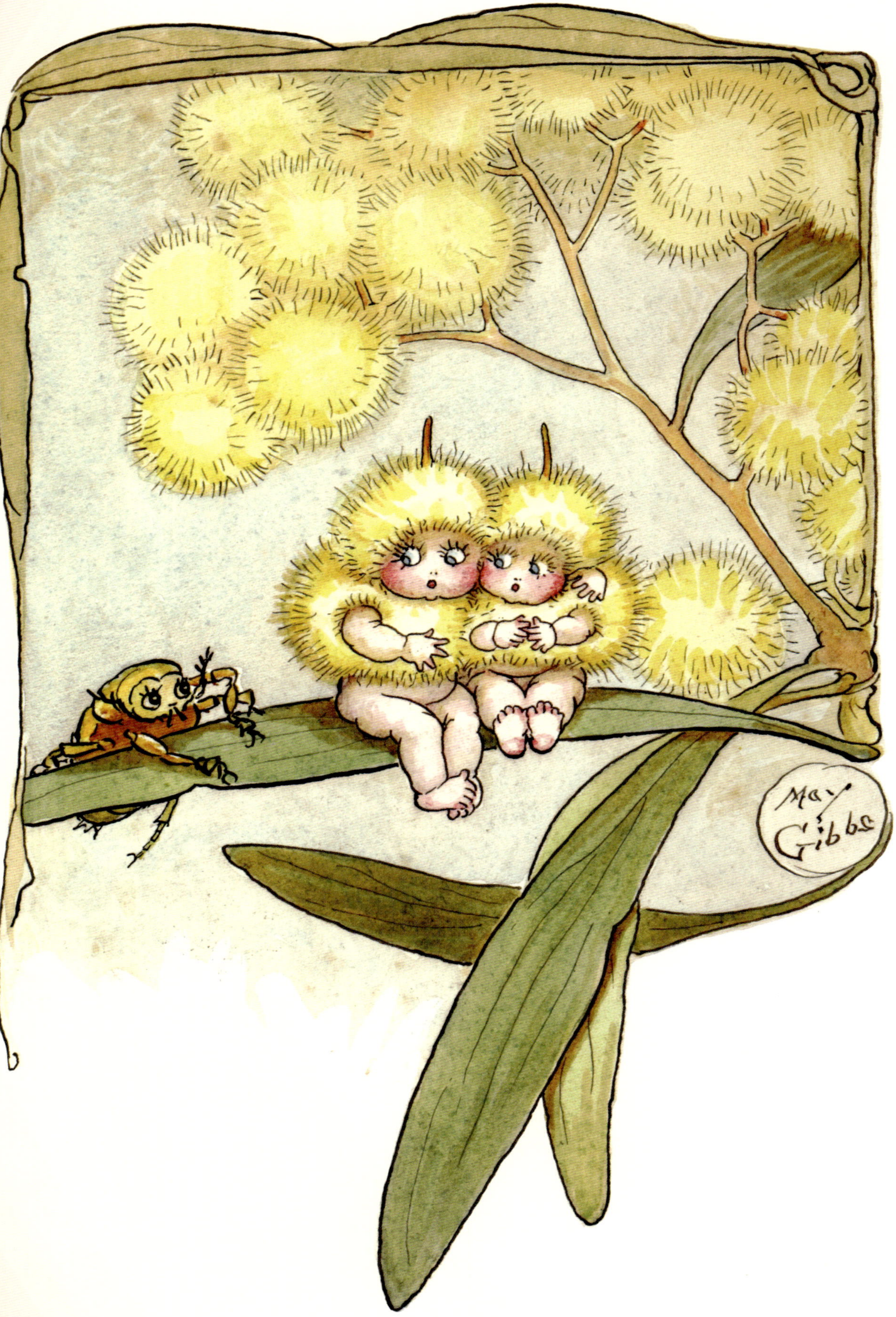
May Gibbs

Wattle Babies

by May Gibbs

When the Caterpillar Canters

Wattle Babies are the sunshine of the Bush. In Winter, when the sky is grey and all the world seems cold, they put on their yellowest clothes and come out, for they have such cheerful hearts.

May Gibbs

Some Visitors Won't Take a Hint

So very good-natured and easy-going are they that many Bush creatures take advantage of them. A mosquito, for instance, will often, in quite a friendly way, make a perfect pest of himself.

May Gibbs

Choosing a Pod for a Boat

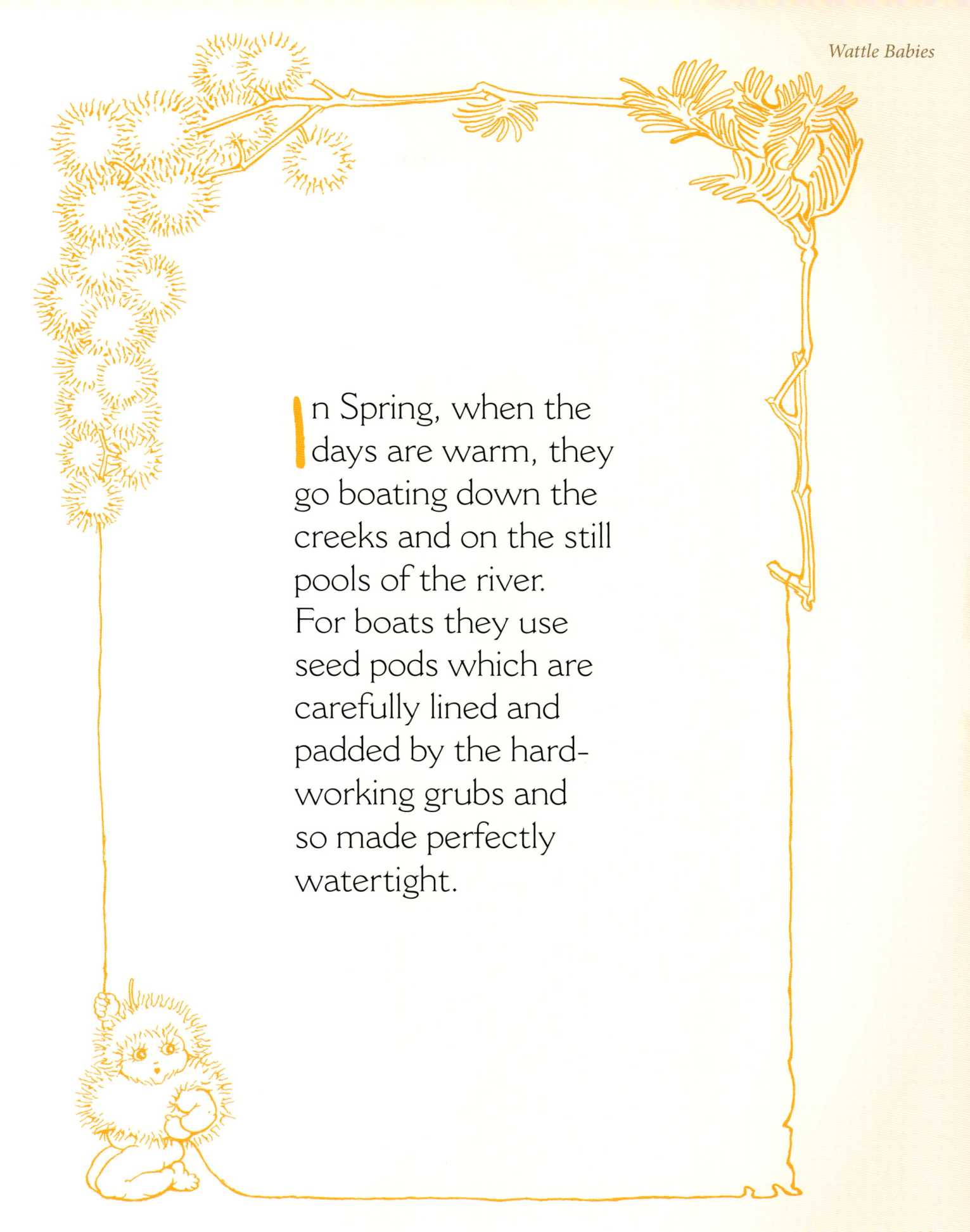

In Spring, when the days are warm, they go boating down the creeks and on the still pools of the river. For boats they use seed pods which are carefully lined and padded by the hard-working grubs and so made perfectly watertight.

May Gibbs

Getting Aboard

Frogs are very friendly with the Wattle Babies—they mind their boats, and teach them how to swim, and show them the dangers of the waterways. Sometimes when there are accidents, if it were not for the frogs, many Wattle Babies would be drowned.

May Gibbs

Not at Home

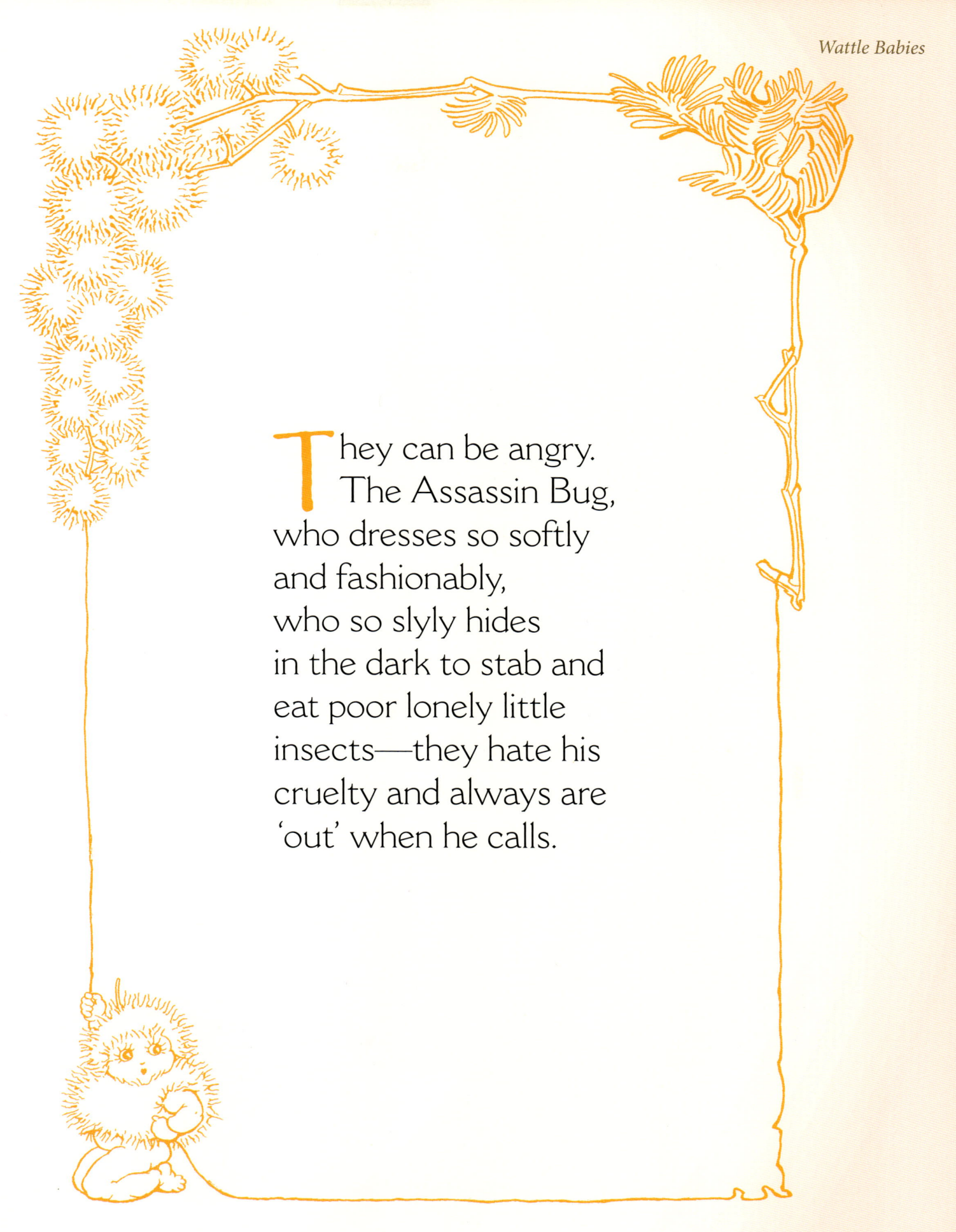

They can be angry. The Assassin Bug, who dresses so softly and fashionably, who so slyly hides in the dark to stab and eat poor lonely little insects—they hate his cruelty and always are 'out' when he calls.

May Gibbs

Picking a Baby

Wattle Babies

Babies grow like buds—together in a spray—and mothers come and pick them when they're big enough. They never choose, but always take the nearest, for some are prettier than others and if the mothers chose the pretty babies how sad it would be for the poor little ugly ones!

May Gibbs

Baby Grubs Make Nice Toys

110

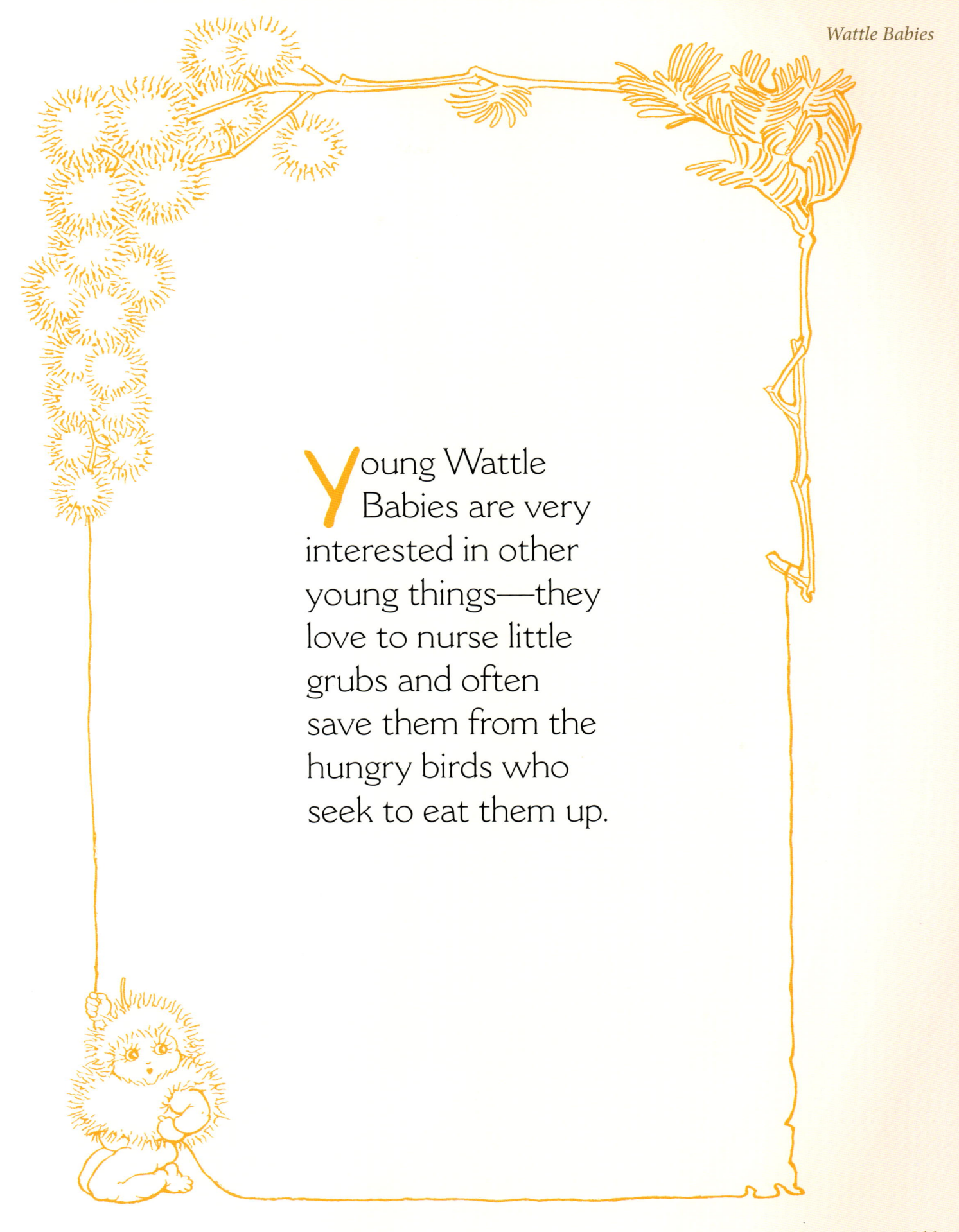

Young Wattle Babies are very interested in other young things—they love to nurse little grubs and often save them from the hungry birds who seek to eat them up.

A Lesson

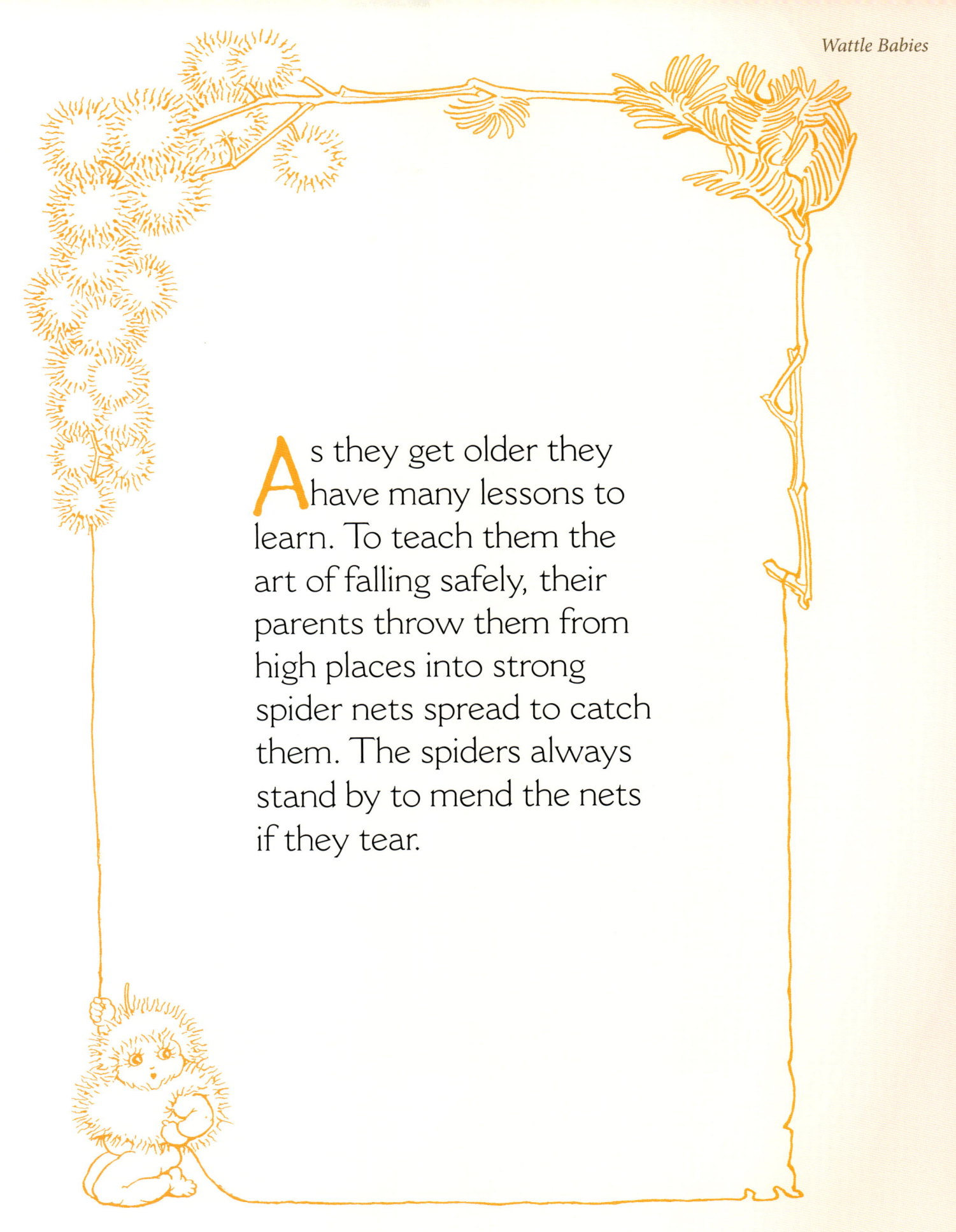

As they get older they have many lessons to learn. To teach them the art of falling safely, their parents throw them from high places into strong spider nets spread to catch them. The spiders always stand by to mend the nets if they tear.

May Gibbs

A Beetlecart

Beetles have no manners and are rather stupid and slow, but their good nature and steadiness make them very useful. Perhaps that is why there are so many beetles on the Wattle Trees.

May Gibbs

Hide and Seek

Baby birds make kind playmates— they are also most useful to sleep under when the nights are chilly.

May Gibbs

A Careful Nurse

Wattle Babies are wiser than humans, for they all dress alike—Boys and Girls, Uncles and Aunts—all in the same convenient clothes. Then again, they don't think—they just live and are happy. If there were no Wattle Babies at all how sad the Bush would be!